100 Read & Sing DeVotions

100 Bible Songs

created by Stephen Elkins

illustrated by Tim O'Connor

A Division of Thomas Nelson Publishers

NASHVILLE   DALLAS   MEXICO CITY   RIO DE JANEIRO

Published in Nashville, Tennessee, by Tommy Nelson. Tommy Nelson is a registered trademark of Thomas Nelson, Inc.

Tommy Nelson, Inc., titles may be purchased in bulk for educational, business, fund-raising, or sales promotional use. For information, please e-mail SpecialMarkets@ThomasNelson.com.

Library of Congress Cataloging-in-Publication Data

Elkins, Stephen.
  100 devotions, 100 Bible songs / created by Stephen Elkins ; illustrated by Tim O'Connor.
     p. cm.
  ISBN 978-1-4003-1716-5 (hardcover with cd)
  1. Christian children—Prayers and devotions. 2. Hymns—Juvenile. I O'Connor, Tim. II. Title.
  BV4870.E449 2011
  242'.62—dc22
                              2011016146

Printed in China

11 12 13 14 RRD 6 5 4 3 2 1

Mfr: RR Donnelley/Shenzhen, China/June 2011—PPO# 120798

Presented To

_____

From

_____

Date

_____

Dear Parents,

Hymns and Bible songs are like "little devotionals" set to music. They can say, *Thank you, Lord, for saving my soul.* They can say *I love you, Lord* as a heart overflows with God's love. And that's what this book is all about—creating an overflowing love for God in the heart of your child. *100 Read & Sing Devotions* takes a deeper look at 100 of these "little devotional" Bible songs, as each song becomes the basis for a devotion. Songs like "Jesus Loves Me" explore the love of Christ. "Deep and Wide" takes a look at the extreme love God has demonstrated. And "This Little Light of Mine" teaches children to grow a bolder faith.

Each devotion begins by singing a song. Then an easy-to-read application is followed by a Bible verse to learn by heart and a prayer to close the devotion. *100 Read & Sing Devotions* will help your child learn to apply God's Word in everyday situations. Whether at school or play, they will discover that God is with them in a real way!

Now you can teach your child to be devoted; that is, to start a lifetime of commitment to God and growing with Him every day. Start now with *100 Read & Sing Devotions!* It is our prayer that your child comes to know God's "Amazing Grace" by "Walking with Jesus." After all, "Everybody Ought to Know" who Jesus is!

Table of Contents

All creatures of our God and King

All creatures of our God and King,
Lift up your voice and with us sing.

Praise! Whether we sing it or shout it, our God is worthy of it! For all the stars He placed in the evening sky, O praise Him! For the silvery moon that lights our way at night, O praise Him! Let the zebra praise Him for his stripes, and the lion for his roar!

Let us praise Him for who He is. He is the Creator of all things. We thank Him for all He has done. *Alleluia* is a Hebrew word that means "Praise the name of God." Have you ever praised God with a song? Let's all praise the Lord by singing, "Alleluia!"

I will praise You, O LORD, with my whole heart.

Psalm 9:1 NKJV

He
is
worthy
of
praise

MY PRAYER FOR TODAY

Lord, I praise You as Creator of all things! Amen.

God Made Me

God made me, God made me.
In my Bible book it says that God made me.

It was God who put the buzz in the bumblebee. It was God who made the flowers in all the colors of the rainbow. He made every creature that lives on the earth. But there's something God made that is even more special. Do you know what it is? He made *you*! He made you just the way you are.

The first man was called Adam. The first woman was Eve. You were created in the image of God, just as they were. And when He created you, He had a special purpose in mind. What is it? You'll have to find out as you grow up. The One who put the buzz in the bumblebee has a purpose for you and for me!

Word Watch

I praise you because I am fearfully and wonderfully made.

Psalm 139:14

GOD MADE ME
CD 1
SONG 2

We **serve** an **awesome** God

MY PRAYER FOR TODAY

Lord, how awesome You must be to have made all things—even me!

Who Built the Ark?

Who built the ark? Noah! Noah!
Who built the ark? Brother Noah built the ark.

We usually think of an ark as a boat. But an ark is any place of shelter in a storm. Noah's ark happened to be a giant boat. It also sheltered his family from the terrible storm that flooded the whole world.

Noah found shelter from the rainstorm in an ark. But there are other kinds of storms. Our families can have problems. Our friends can be unkind. Kids can tease us and hurt our feelings. But be glad . . . we have an "ark" from these storms too! God is our shelter in stormy times. Depend on Him when you are troubled. Cast your cares on Him because He is your ark.

WHO BUILT THE ARK?
CD 1
SONG 3

The
Lord
is
my
"ark"

Word Watch

For You have been a shelter for me,
a strong tower from the enemy.

Psalm 61:3 NKJV

MY PRAYER FOR TODAY

Lord, You are my "ark"; You are my shelter
in the storm. I love You, Lord. Amen.

Is Anything Too Hard for the Lord?

Have a little faith, believe it's true,
And you will find there's nothing He can't do.

God made a promise to Abraham: his children would outnumber the stars in the sky. But Abraham and Sarah were very old. Sarah laughed at the thought of having children at her age. But God spoke and said, "Is anything too hard for the LORD?" At age ninety, Sarah had a little baby boy named Isaac.

The story of Abraham and Sarah teaches us to keep our eyes on the promise, not on the problem. There is nothing our God cannot do. He can heal the sick, raise the dead, calm a sea, and even make blind eyes see! So why would Abraham and Sarah doubt God's promise of children? They did not understand how great God is! Nothing is too hard for Him! He is able to keep His promises to you.

Word Watch

Is anything too hard for the LORD?

Genesis 18:14

~

All **things** are **possible** for **God**

MY PRAYER FOR TODAY

Lord, there is nothing too hard for You to do! You are my God. Amen.

God Is So Good

God is so good, He's so good to me!

Isaac married a beautiful girl named Rebekah. They were about to get a big surprise! Rebekah was going to have twin boys. God is so good! But remember, God's goodness doesn't always mean a good time. Daniel faced a lions' den. And Jonah faced a whale. But God was still good!

Sometimes things happen that don't seem fair, and we can't understand why. But remember, the Bible says *all things* work together for the good of those who love God. Is there something in your life that you can't understand? It will work out for good . . . because God is so good!

Word Watch

The LORD is good to all.

Psalm 145:9

God
is
good
to
me

MY PRAYER FOR TODAY

Lord, You have been good to me.
Help me to be a blessing to others. Amen.

Whisper a Prayer

*Whisper a prayer
To keep your heart in tune.*

I once had an old guitar that I could not get in tune. The more I turned those tuning keys, the worse it sounded. In despair, I took my clanging guitar to a master musician. He listened to each string very carefully. Then he began to tune each one until that clanging guitar sounded like a new one. It just needed a master's touch to produce the right sound.

Sometimes our hearts can get "out of tune." We can get discouraged or even angry about something. We may try to fix it ourselves. But when nothing changes the "clang" in our heart, that's the time to go to the Master in prayer. Prayer changes things. It's like getting a spiritual tune-up.

Word Watch

Pray without ceasing.

1 Thessalonians 5:17 NKJV

Prayer
changes
things

MY PRAYER FOR TODAY

Lord, I want my heart to be in tune with Yours! Amen.

We Are Climbing Jacob's Ladder

Behold, I am with you and will watch o'er you;
Soldiers of the cross.

As Jacob slept, he dreamed of angels. They were walking on a stairway up to heaven. The Lord spoke to Jacob in a dream, making this promise, "Behold, I am with you and will watch over you." And that is still the promise of God to His children today.

The same God who created the earth; who parted a mighty sea before Moses; who protected Shadrach, Meshach, and Abednego from the flames; who closed the mouths of lions and opened blind eyes with a touch—the same almighty God has promised to watch over *you*! So do not be afraid. The God who watched over Jacob will watch over you.

Word Watch

I am with you and will watch
over you wherever you go.

Genesis 28:15

~

The
Lord
is
with
me

MY PRAYER FOR TODAY

Lord, thank You for watching over me throughout
the day and night. I love You, Lord! Amen.

21

Joseph's Coat of Many Colors

 Many colors, many colors, Joseph had a coat of many colors.

Joseph's father gave him a beautiful coat of many colors. His brothers were very jealous. Then Joseph told them of his dream: they would one day bow down before him. His brothers were very angry. All the unkind things that Joseph's brothers did started with a jealous heart.

Jealousy is not a good thing according to the Bible. We are to be content with what God has given us. Sometimes people do things we can't do. They get things we wish we had. In those moments, we must be careful that we don't become jealous or envious. Don't let jealousy or envy make its way into your heart. Be content with all that God has given you!

Word Watch

Let us not become conceited, provoking and envying each other.

Galatians 5:26

~

Let
us
be
content

MY PRAYER FOR TODAY

Lord, teach me to be content
with what You have given me. Amen.

This Is the Day

This is the day the Lord has made.
Let us rejoice and be glad in it.

Have you ever considered all the things God has done to make a day? First, God created light. Next, God created planet Earth. He set Earth spinning around the sun, which He also created. And while all of this is moving through millions of galaxies full of other suns and stars and planets, you lay sleeping in your bed.

Suddenly, the alarm clock goes off. Your dog jumps up and licks you on the face! You open your sleepy eyes, and say, "This is the day the Lord has made!" The next time you wake up grumpy, remember that God went to an awful lot of trouble to make your day. So rejoice and be glad!

Word Watch

This is the day the LORD has made; let us rejoice and be glad in it.

Psalm 118:24 HCSB

Rejoice
in
the
Lord
always

MY PRAYER FOR TODAY

Lord, thank You for making today
and for giving me eyes to see it. Amen.

The Fruit of the Spirit

 The fruit of the spirit is love, joy, and peace

What kind of fruit grows on an apple tree? Apples, of course! An apple tree only produces apples. It cannot produce oranges, even if it wanted to. Likewise, when we become Christians, Jesus produces "fruit" in us. It's called the "fruit of the Spirit." This fruit is the love, joy, and peace that only He can produce in us!

Many people try to find lasting joy and peace without loving Jesus. They think that other things in this world can replace His love. We know that apple trees can only produce apples. And only Jesus can produce in us the kind of fruit that fills a heart with love, joy, and peace!

Word Watch

But the fruit of the Spirit is love, joy, peace . . .

Galatians 5:22

Jesus
fills
us
with
love

MY PRAYER FOR TODAY

Lord, I am attached to Jesus. Thank You
for producing fruit in me. Amen.

God Will Take Care of You

No matter what may be the test,
God will take care of you.

Pharaoh said, "No more Jewish baby boys in my kingdom!" What was a mother to do? Moses' mother chose to trust God. She placed her baby in a basket. All her love and trust in God went with baby Moses as he floated away down the Nile River.

You can trust God too. To trust is to depend on God. To trust is to believe that God loves you and will take care of you. Trusting God begins with little things. As your faith grows, you learn to trust Him with things you treasure most. Baby Moses was found by an Egyptian princess. He was saved because his mother trusted God to take care of him. God will take care of you too!

Word Watch

O Lord, you will keep us safe and protect us.

Psalm 12:7

The
Lord
keeps
me
safe

MY PRAYER FOR TODAY

Lord, may I trust You more with each passing day. Amen.

29

I Am Bound for the Promised Land

O who will come and go with me?
I am bound for the Promised Land.

God's people were finally free after four hundred years of bondage in Egypt! They were going home to a place called the promised land! It would take forty years to get there. But God would provide all along the way. He would even make a way through the Red Sea!

God promised Moses an earthly land. God kept that promise. As Christians, we have a different promised land. It's not here on Earth. It's a promise called heaven. Heaven is where God lives, and there is only one way to get there. No, not through the Red Sea, but through a red-stained cross. Jesus made the only way to heaven! With Him, we are bound for the promised land!

Jesus answered, "I am the way and the truth and the life. No one comes to the Father except through me."

John 14:6

Jesus is the **Way**

MY PRAYER FOR TODAY

Lord, I am bound for the promised land of heaven because I trust in Jesus. Amen.

This Is My Commandment

This is my commandment,
That you love one another.

God called Moses to the top of a mountain and said, "I am the LORD your God." (Exodus 20:2) Then He gave Moses the Ten Commandments. Four of the commandments taught us to respect God. Six taught us to respect each other. There was one problem; no one could keep all of the commandments all of the time.

That is why Jesus was called to the top of a mountain too . . . Mount Calvary. He was able to keep all the commandments. He lived a perfect life. And on that mountain He gave up His perfect life for you and me. He said, "A new command I give you: Love one another. As I have loved you, so you must love one another." Is there anyone able to keep the commandments? None but Jesus!

Word Watch

A new command I give you: Love one another.

John 13:34

~

God's
commandments
are
good

MY PRAYER FOR TODAY

Lord, I have not kept Your commandments.
Thank You, Jesus, for keeping them for me. Amen.

Little Jobs

Whoever can be trusted with very little,
Can also be trusted with very much.

Washing twelve cars a day wasn't a lot of fun. But it was my job, so I did my best. I didn't know my boss was watching me so closely. He needed someone who could be trusted to do a bigger job. Since I did a little job well, I was promoted to the big job!

It works the same in God's kingdom. Today, you might help a neighbor rake the leaves; you may help teach a Sunday school class. Then someday, you may teach on a mission field in a faraway country. Why? Because you were faithful to do a little job, which led to a bigger and more responsible job. Do you have a little job that you're doing for the Lord? Then do it well! Little jobs will lead to more responsible jobs! God needs a good worker!

Word Watch

Whoever can be trusted with very little can also be trusted with much.

Luke 16:10

Be **faithful** to the **task**

MY PRAYER FOR TODAY

Lord, help me to do the little jobs You give me well. Amen.

Joshua Fought the Battle of Jericho

And the walls came tumbling down!

Joshua stood before the tall, strong walls of Jericho. He must have wondered how he would win the battle. But God gave him a plan. For six days, Joshua would march his army around the walls of Jericho. Then, on the seventh day, they would shout! It certainly didn't seem like a good plan. But Joshua and the people obeyed the Lord. When they did, those walls tumbled down!

Why did God ask Joshua to shout at a wall? He wanted His people to have faith in Him. He wanted them to understand that *His way* of doing things is not like their way. He still wants us to trust in His ways. Do you have a giant problem? Trust God's ways, and watch those problems tumble down.

Word Watch

As the heavens are higher than the earth, so are my ways higher than your ways and my thoughts than your thoughts.

Isaiah 55:9

God's **way** is **always** best

MY PRAYER FOR TODAY

Lord, Your ways are the ways of the Spirit.
Help me listen with my heart. Amen.

children, Obey Your Parents

 Children, obey your parents in the Lord,
For this is right.

God tells us how a family should work in the Bible. Children are to respect and obey their parents. The word *obey* means to understand and to do what you are asked to do.

This Bible verse also says that you should "honor your father and your mother" (Exodus 20:12). To honor your parents is to show them proper respect. How do we do this?

R—be *Reliable*
E—*Excel* by doing your best
S—be *Self-controlled*
P—be *Patient* with brothers and sisters
E—be a good *Example*
C—be *Christlike* in all you do, and . . .
T—be *Thankful*

Obedience begins with R-E-S-P-E-C-T. Show your parents respect. That's the way to obey!

Word Watch

He who obeys instruction guards his life.

Proverbs 19:16

~

Honor God and your **parents**

MY PRAYER FOR TODAY

Lord, teach me to obey and honor my parents. Amen.

When I Am Afraid

When I am afraid, I will trust in You.
I will trust in You, O Lord my God.

The Bible tells us about men and women of courage. Deborah showed great courage by going into battle! People with courage do the right thing, even though they are afraid. They do not let fear stop them. Deborah may have feared the enemies of Israel, but she showed great courage. She faced the enemy with bravery.

Where did she find all this courage? God was her strength. She knew God was faithful! Deborah obeyed God, and He led Israel to victory. When the battle was won, Deborah celebrated by singing. She praised the Lord for their victory.

When I am afraid, I will trust in you.

Psalm 56:3

~

God
is
my
strength

MY PRAYER FOR TODAY

Lord, when I am afraid, help me to have courage. Amen.

God Is My Strength

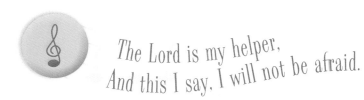

The Lord is my helper,
And this I say, I will not be afraid.

Samson was very strong. His strength was a gift from God. He was to live a holy life. "Holy" means to be set apart from people who do bad things. He was to obey God and do good things. But Samson was not holy. Soon, he found himself chained between two stone pillars, where his enemies mocked him and his God.

Have you ever done something that was wrong because everyone else was doing it? Samson did, and look what happened to him! God wants us to be holy too. What did Samson do when he disobeyed? He prayed for strength. You can too!

Word Watch

Be holy because I, the LORD your God, am holy.

Leviticus 19:2

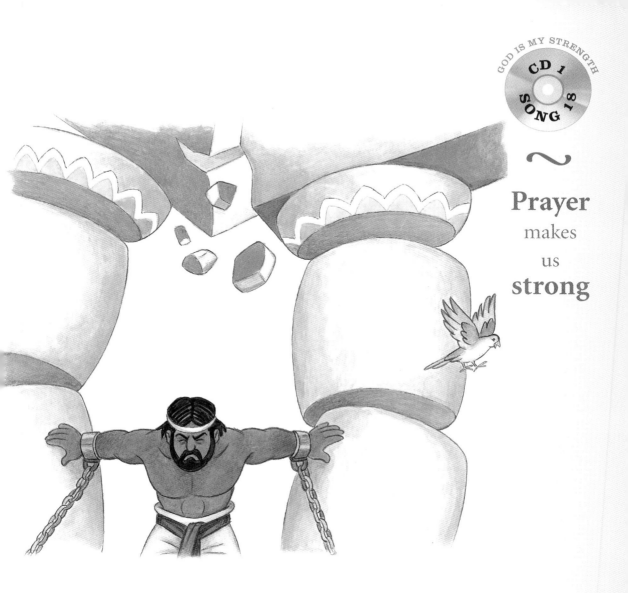

Prayer
makes
us
strong

MY PRAYER FOR TODAY

Lord, help me to set apart my time, talents,
and treasures to serve You. Amen.

Walking with Jesus

For I am walking in the sunlight, walking in the shadow,
Walking with Jesus alone.

What does it mean to walk with Jesus? We do what He would do and say what He would say. And that's not easy! Sometimes our friends do and say things that Jesus would not. That's why the song says "walking with Jesus alone." But you're never really alone if Jesus is with you!

When others do bad things, tell them about Paul. He did bad things, but then he started walking with Jesus. When people say bad things, tell them about Peter. He said some bad things, but then he walked back to Jesus. When people go places they shouldn't go, tell them about Jonah. He disobeyed, but then he walked . . . oops . . . I mean, swam back to God. Remember, it's better to walk with Jesus than run with the world!

Word Watch

Let us walk in the light of the LORD.

Isaiah 2:5

~

Jesus
is
with
you

MY PRAYER FOR TODAY

Lord, may I always walk with Jesus,
even if I have to walk alone. Amen.

The Lord Is Good to Me

He cares for those who trust in Him.
He cares for you and me.

How many times should we pray for God's help? One time? Ten times? The Bible tells of a heartbroken woman named Hannah. She had been praying for a baby for years. How many times had she prayed? No one knows for sure, but one night she cried out in prayer, "Lord, bless me with a child." When the time was right, a baby named Samuel was born.

Hannah's prayer had been answered on God's timetable, not her own. Sometimes we have to wait on the Lord. We must believe that He hears. We must wait for His answer, and know God hears and will answer. That's real faith! Are you waiting on God to answer a prayer? Rest assured, He will answer you at just the right time!

Word Watch

Wait for the LORD.

Psalm 27:14

God
answers
prayer

MY PRAYER FOR TODAY

Lord, You have heard my prayer. Now I
will wait on You to answer. Amen.

Wherever He Leads, I'll Go

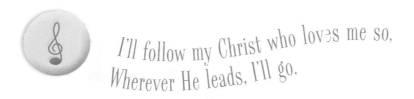

I'll follow my Christ who loves me so,
Wherever He leads, I'll go.

Jesus said that to be a good leader, you must learn to follow. You must "take up a cross" and follow Him. What does that mean? "Taking up a cross" means that we do the things Jesus did—like helping a friend, obeying your parents, going to church, or praying for a sick neighbor.

But you can't "take up" a cross until you "lay down" something else. What do we lay down? We lay down selfish things and take up the things God wants. Have you taken up a cross? Are you doing the things Jesus did? Are you praying? Then you are becoming a leader. Keep following Jesus!

Word Watch

You must follow me.

John 21:22

WHEREVER HE LEADS, I'LL GO
CD 1
SONG 21

Follow Jesus **every** day

MY PRAYER FOR TODAY

Lord, I want to be a good leader for Jesus.
Teach me to follow Him more. Amen.

Let My Little Light Shine

 Every day, every day, every day in every way, I'm gonna let my little light shine.

Jesus said that we should be a light for Him. How do we let our light shine for Jesus? You show others what it means to be a Christian. You can't light a candle in a dark room and not see it. When you are kind to others, you shine for Jesus!

People will see your "light," and they'll want to be around you. Then you can tell them why you shine. Tell them about God's love, and how He sent Jesus to show us the way to live. It's like a lightbulb coming on! Is there someone you know who is living in darkness? Just let your little light shine!

Word Watch

You are the light of the world.

Matthew 5:14

The **Lord** will **light** your **way**

MY PRAYER FOR TODAY

Lord, I want my little light to shine for You. Amen.

Everybody Ought to Know

 He's the lily of the valley. He's the bright and morning star. He's the fairest of ten thousand.

Preachers tell people what they ought to know. They ought to know that Jesus is Lord, which means the One we serve. They ought to know that Jesus is the Son of God. The wise men called Jesus the King of the Jews. Peter called Jesus the Christ, which means the One who gives us what we need. What do we need? Salvation! His very name, *Jesus*, means "God saves." The angel said to Mary, "This Jesus will *save* the people."

And that's what everybody ought to know. Jesus is Lord and Savior; the One we serve, who gives us the salvation we need! Do you know people who ought to know who Jesus is? Go tell them!

Word Watch

Now this is eternal life: that they may know you, the only true God, and Jesus Christ, whom you have sent.

John 17:3

~

Tell **everyone** about God's **love**

MY PRAYER FOR TODAY

Lord, everybody in the whole world needs to know who Jesus is. I want to tell them, Lord. Amen.

Train Up

*Train up a child in the way she should go,
And when she is older, she will not depart from it.*

Little birds sit in a nest. They are high up in their treetop home and the ground is way down below! But they watch and learn as mama bird zooms through the air. She encourages them daily to step out and fly. Somehow she knows that God will take care of them.

Like little birds, you were designed by God too. Watch your parents. Learn from them. Listen to their instruction, and apply the wise lessons they teach you. Let your parents train you up to be a child of God! Do you think you can do that? Yes, you can!

Word Watch

Train up a child in the way he should go.

Proverbs 22:6 KJV

Be
a
child
of
God

MY PRAYER FOR TODAY

Lord, help me to honor and obey my parents
as they seek to train me up in the Lord. Amen.

Only a Boy Named David

And one little stone went up in the air,
And the giant came tumbling down.

Goliath stood nearly ten feet tall. He was covered with armor from head to toe. He shouted out to the army of Israel, "Come fight me!" But no one would fight the giant. Goliath began to mock God. When David heard this, he walked out to face Goliath. He said, "You come against me with a sword and spear. But I come against you in the name of the God of Israel!"

Strength is not measured by the size of a little boy or girl. It is measured by the size of their God. How big is your God? Is He bigger than Goliath? Yes, He is! The next time you face a giant problem, don't worry. Ask God to be your strength. Then praise Him with a song!

But You are holy, O You Who dwell in the praises . . . of Israel.

Psalm 22:3 AMP

The
Lord
answers
giant
prayers

MY PRAYER FOR TODAY

Lord, when problems become "giant problems,"
I will seek You in prayer and praise You in song. Amen.

What a Mighty Hand

What a mighty hand, a hand protecting me,
What a mighty hand has He.

Elijah stood on Mount Carmel. With him were two hundred prophets of the false god Baal. They were there to find out which "god" was the one true almighty God. The prophets of Baal called out, "Send fire from heaven." But nothing happened. Then Elijah called to the one true God of Israel. A great ball of fire fell from heaven. Elijah's God was mighty!

Understanding who God is, and who we are not, is an important part of growing up. When we see that God is real and His power is great, our faith begins to grow. We are humbled by all that God can do. What does it mean to be humbled? You begin to see the needs you have, and you come to God to ask Him to supply them. Elijah's God is our God, and He is mighty!

Word Watch

Humble yourselves, therefore, under God's mighty hand.

1 Peter 5:6

The
Lord
is
mighty

MY PRAYER FOR TODAY

Lord, may I come to You in humility,
for You are great and mighty. Amen.

WHAT A MIGHTY HAND
CD 1
SONG 26

What a Friend We Have in Jesus

Jesus knows our every weakness;
Take it to the Lord in prayer.

They call him man's best friend. He's a four-legged fur ball who barks at cats and licks you in the face with that big, sloppy tongue! Dogs are a lot of fun and make great friends. But the Bible says our very best friend is Jesus!

Jesus said He calls us His friends! Can you imagine . . . the One who walked on water, who healed the sick and calmed the sea, wants to be your friend? What do friends like to do most? Get together and talk! They talk about joys and sorrows, about hopes and dreams. So think of Jesus as your very best friend. Talk to Him every day in prayer!

Word Watch

I have called you friends, for everything that I learned
from my Father I have made known to you.

John 15:15

Jesus
calls
us
friends

MY PRAYER FOR TODAY

Lord, You are my best friend. Help me spend more time with You in prayer. Amen.

I Will Deliver You

Call upon Me in the day of trouble;
I will deliver you.

As a boy, I used to deliver newspapers. Every morning before school, I would pick up the papers on the corner and deliver them to each house in the neighborhood. They called me the delivery boy. *Deliver* means to move something from one place to another. My job was to move the papers from where they were to where the people wanted them to be.

Naaman needed to be delivered. He was very sick. Elisha told him God's plan, "Dip in the river seven times, and you will be delivered." God was about to move something. Naaman obeyed and was delivered. God moved Naaman's disease out of his body and washed it away in the water. Do you need to be delivered from something? Sadness . . . or trouble? Call upon the Lord. He will deliver you!

Word Watch

Call upon me in the day of trouble; I will deliver you and you will honor me.

Psalm 50:15

The
Lord
is
my
deliverer

MY PRAYER FOR TODAY
Lord, thank You for being my deliverer. Amen.

The Jabez Prayer

Father, come bless me, bless me indeed.
All of the honor and glory I'll give back to Thee.

The Bible says that Jabez was a good man. One day, he prayed to God. Jabez wanted something big. And he wanted it for all the right reasons. He asked God to make his ministry bigger, so he could tell more people about God's love and mighty deeds. "Bless me," he said, "and let me tell more people about God's love."

Only God can see inside our hearts. He not only hears our prayers; He knows why we're praying. Sometimes we ask for selfish things. That can make God sad. But when we ask unselfishly, God is pleased. Jabez wanted more *from* God so he could give more *to* God. Are you asking for the right reasons, like Jabez did?

Word Watch

Man looks at the outward appearance, but the LORD looks at the heart.

I Samuel 16:7

Only
God
sees
the
heart

MY PRAYER FOR TODAY

Lord, I want my motives to be right.
May I only ask for things that please You. Amen.

Where You Go, I Will Go

Friends are friends eternally,
That's the way a friend should be.

The Bible has a lot to say about friendship. Solomon wrote that a friend loves at all times. Fair-weather friends walk away when things get tough. But real friends love all the time, no matter what. Ruth was a real friend to Naomi. When the famine was over, Naomi decided to go back home. It was a long journey. Ruth would help Naomi make the difficult trip home.

Friendship might have us give up our time, or something we own. It might require a little extra work. But remember, *love* is an action verb. When we love, we must do something. Jesus loved us by doing something. He gave His life for His friends! Is there someone you know who needs a friend? Remember, a friend loves at *all* times!

A friend loves at all times.

Proverbs 17:17

WHERE YOU GO, I WILL GO
CD 1
SONG 30

Share God's **love** with **friends**

MY PRAYER FOR TODAY

Lord, I want to be a better friend to others.
Help me share Your love with my friends. Amen.

I've Got Peace Like a River

I've got peace like a river in my soul.

Nolan and Julia had just pushed away from the dock in their canoe. The river was smooth and the sky was clear. They hadn't gone very far when Nolan realized they forgot something very important. They forgot their life preservers on the dock. They had to go back!

Life preservers keep us safe and give us peace of mind. They're always there in times of trouble. Jesus is like that. He's always there in times of trouble. Have you ever forgotten about Jesus? He can save us when we fall into trouble. Jesus saves, and He gives us peace He's our lifesaver!

Word Watch

Jesus said, "Peace be with you!"

John 20:21

Jesus
gives
us
peace

MY PRAYER FOR TODAY

Lord, let me never forget about Jesus and
the peace He gives to those who trust Him. Amen.

I Wanna Throw Up My Hands

 I wanna throw up my hands and praise the Lord!

If God is Lord of *all*, shouldn't He be praised in *all* places? Most certainly, YES! When you lie down to sleep, praise the Lord for His watch care. When you're playing ball in the park, praise the Lord for your hands. When you're running in the backyard, praise the Lord for your feet! Give God praise for everything! But do we do that?

In ancient times, soldiers would raise their hands to praise God for the victory. They didn't wait till they got home or went to church. They praised the Lord right there on the battlefield. Anytime is the right time, anyplace is the right place to praise the Lord. Throw up your hands and praise the Lord right now!

Word Watch

I will praise you as long as I live, and in your name I will lift up my hands.

Psalm 63:4

~

Lift your **hands** in **praise**

MY PRAYER FOR TODAY

Lord, I will lift my hands in praise of who
You are and what You have done. Amen.

73

If My People Pray

Blessings are a-comin'
If we walk by faith and do it.

Some small words have big meanings . . . like the words *if* and *then*. Has your mother ever said, "*If* you clean your room, *then* you may have ice cream"? Or maybe, "*If* you do your homework, *then* we'll make popcorn"?

God used these little words in this Bible verse. He wanted to see a change in His people. He said, "*If* you will humble yourselves, pray, seek me, and turn from bad things . . . *then* I will hear your prayers, forgive the wrong, and make your nation strong again." Four things make a nation strong being humble, praying, seeking God, and turning from bad things. Can we do it? *If* we can, *then* God will change things!

Word Watch

If my people, who are called by my name, will humble themselves and

pray and seek my face and turn from their wicked ways, then will I hear

from heaven and will forgive their sin and will heal their land.

2 Chronicles 7:14

~

God
makes
a
nation
strong

MY PRAYER FOR TODAY

Lord, a nation is made great when people
humble themselves, pray, seek You, and repent.
May our nation do these things. Amen.

Give, and It Will Be Given to You

It will be poured into your lap,
For with the measure you use, it will be measured to you.

Some people have a misunderstanding of who God is. They think God is a "meanie" who takes away our fun. But nothing could be further from the truth. Our God is loving and caring. Instead of taking away, He longs to give.

He promises, "Give to others, and I will give back to you more than you ever imagined." He compares His giving to a big container. It holds a "good measure." He presses down what He's put inside so He can give even more. That doesn't sound like a meanie to me. God is giving! Would you like to be a better giver? Remember, you can't outgive the One who has given everything for you!

Word Watch

Give, and it will be given to you.

Luke 6:38

Our
God
is
giving

MY PRAYER FOR TODAY

Lord, I know You are a giving God.
Help me to be a more giving person. Thank You. Amen.

Building Others Up

We're building others' confidence,
That's what we all should do!

The walls around Jerusalem were in terrible condition. They needed to be rebuilt, and Nehemiah knew he was just the man for the job. Building a wall can take a long time. Tearing one down can take only a moment.

The same is true with people. It only takes a moment for unkind words to tear a person down. The Bible calls this "unwholesome talk." Instead of building up a person, unwholesome talk tears him or her down. Let's be like Nehemiah. Let's build others up, not tear them down. Use kind words as Jesus would do, to build others up!

Word Watch

Do not let any unwholesome talk come out of your mouths.

Ephesians 4:29

~

Kind **words build** others **up**

MY PRAYER FOR TODAY

Lord, I want to be a Nehemiah.
Help me to always build others up in the Lord. Amen.

For Such a Time as This

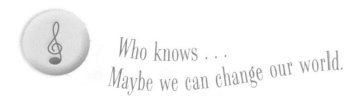

*Who knows . . .
Maybe we can change our world.*

Esther was beautiful. God made her that way for a special purpose. She would become queen of Persia at just the right time. When the Jews came under attack, Esther was there! She stopped bad men from hurting God's people.

In what way are you special? Are you good at math? Do you like to color? Do you run fast, or would you rather sit in a chair and read a book? Whether you're smart, or strong, or artistic, God created you just the way you are to do something special. Be patient At just the right time, God will show you what to do!

Word Watch

And who knows but that you have come
to royal position for such a time as this?

Esther 4:14

~

God
has
work
for
me

MY PRAYER FOR TODAY

Lord, I know that You have prepared a work for me to do.
Help me to do it when that day comes. Amen.

Don't Get caught in the Net

*Don't get caught in the net the devil throws at you.
Put your trust in Jesus, and you'll make it through!*

There was a groundhog in my garden eating all my beets. But I like beets too! So I bought a trap and filled it with fresh beets. When he went in to get a tasty treat—*bam!* The trapdoor closed. I took him to the woods and let him go. Problem solved!

If you want to get a groundhog away from a garden, beets will do the job. But sometimes we can get away from the Lord. How do we get trapped like that? Maybe a bad friend or a Web site causes problems. Don't get caught in a net. That's for fish and butterflies . . . and groundhogs that eat my beets!

Word Watch

God will grant . . . that they will come to their senses and escape
from the trap of the devil, who has taken them captive to do his will.

2 Timothy 2:25-26

DON'T GET CAUGHT IN THE NET

CD 1
SONG 37

Stay **close** to the **Lord**

MY PRAYER FOR TODAY

Lord, keep me close to You so that I will not get caught in the devil's trap. Amen.

Come, Let us Bow Down and Worship

He is the Lord of lords.
Before Him there really is no other.

Job was a man who pleased God in every way. One day, Satan appeared before God and got permission to test Job. Bad things began to happen to Job. His oxen and donkeys were stolen. His servants were killed. Fire destroyed all his sheep and camels. Job fell to his knees and prayed, "It is the Lord who gives; it is the Lord who takes away. Praise the name of the Lord!" Job did not blame God for his trouble.

Why do bad things happen to good people? Sometimes, God may test us. Other times, He is building our character. But all the time, God loves us and deserves our worship. Come, let us bow down and worship our mighty God!

Word Watch

The LORD gave and the LORD has taken away;

may the name of the LORD be praised.

Job 1:21

COME, LET US BOW DOWN AND WORSHIP
CD 1
SONG 38

~

Worship the **Lord**, no matter what

MY PRAYER FOR TODAY

Lord, may I worship You no matter what, in good times and bad. Amen.

Dry Bones

O, Ezekiel connected dem dry bones.
Now hear the word of the Lord!

It was a frightening dream! Ezekiel stood in a valley filled with bones. Then he heard the voice of the Lord say, "Can these bones live?" Suddenly, there came the rattling sound of bones coming back to life! Then God told Ezekiel the meaning of the dream: "My people are hopeless. They think they are dead, like these bones. Tell them I am going to restore them." So Ezekiel shouted, "Dry bones can live! All things are possible with God!"

And it's true! All things are possible with our mighty God. Is there something in your life that needs God's touch? If God can make dry bones live, He can do the impossible for you! Have great faith and believe God!

Word Watch

With God all things are possible.

Matthew 19:26

Have
great
faith

MY PRAYER FOR TODAY

Lord, may I never forget that all
things are possible with You. Amen.

Onward, Christian Soldiers

Christ, the royal Master, leads against the foe;
Forward into battle, see His banner go!

Have you ever watched the evening news and seen pictures from a war? The Bible records many wars and battles. Rahab once helped Joshua win the battle of Jericho by helping two of his spies escape the enemy.

But there is another kind of battle. It's a war with an unseen enemy who fights for our hearts and souls. Who is this enemy? He's called the "evil one" in the Bible. His desire is to see us defeated. His weapons are selfishness and pride. But our weapon is the Bible. It tells us Jesus has already won this battle. He defeated our enemy on the cross! Would you like to be a soldier in the Lord's army? Basic training begins with trusting Jesus. He is our defense. He is our victory!

Put on the full armor of God so that you can take your stand against the devil's schemes.

Ephesians 6:11

The **Lord** is our **victory**

MY PRAYER FOR TODAY

Lord, make me a good soldier in Your army.
Teach me how to tell of the victory of Jesus! Amen.

Lean Not on Your Own Understanding

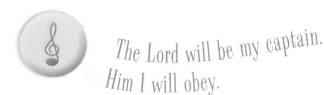

*The Lord will be my captain.
Him I will obey.*

Everyone was commanded to either worship the gold statue, or be cast into a fire. Everyone obeyed the king except Shadrach, Meshach, and Abednego. They would not worship the statue. They said, "God is able to save us. But even if He does not, we will not worship the image of gold." They knew God was mighty, and if He chose to save them, they would be saved. They would trust God and leave the outcome to Him.

Do you believe God can be trusted? Do you believe He is able to help you? Then do what's right, and leave the outcome to Him. Three men were cast into the fire, but a fourth man appeared. The Lord was with them, even in the fire. He is with you too!

Word Watch

Trust in the LORD with all your heart.

Proverbs 3:5

CD 1
SONG 14
LEAN NOT ON YOUR OWN UNDERSTANDING

Worship **God** alone

MY PRAYER FOR TODAY

Lord, I know I must learn to trust You. Help me never to worship anyone or anything but You. Amen.

Praise Him, Praise Him

Praise Him, praise Him, all ye little children. God is love. God is love.

Sometimes we hear people sing, "God is love," and wonder what it means. The word used in the Bible for "love" is *agape*. This is the love God has for His people. It's the kind of love His people have for God and for each other. It's love with hands and feet. It helps those who cannot help themselves. Jesus said to love our enemies. Only God's love can help us do that!

God's kind of love deserves our praise! That's because God's love is an action love! He loved us so much that He gave His Son, Jesus, to save us. He supplies our needs each and every day. So we sing, "Praise Him, praise Him!" God is love.

Word Watch

I will sing praise to Your name, O Most High.

Psalm 9:2 NKJV

~
God
is
love

MY PRAYER FOR TODAY

Lord, for all that You are and for all that
You have done, I praise You! Amen.

I See the Moon

I see the moon and the moon sees me.
God bless the moon and God bless me.

When you kneel down beside your bed to pray, something very special happens. You come into the presence of God. And because of who He is, you kneel. Kneeling is a sign you are humbling yourself. You kneel before God to say, "You are great; You are mighty." It shows God how much you respect Him.

Then you begin to talk to the same God Moses prayed to in his time of trouble. You praise the same God David praised when he was happy. And if you look up, you see the same moon Jesus saw as He prayed in the garden. Yes, God made that moon. And God blesses all who are humble.

Word Watch

A man can receive only what is given him from heaven.

John 3:27

God
bless
me

MY PRAYER FOR TODAY

Lord, all blessings can be traced to Your hand.
Thank You, Lord, for blessing me! Amen.

Give Thanks to the Lord

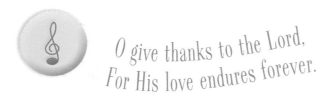

O give thanks to the Lord,
For His love endures forever.

What is the biggest number you can think of? You may think of a number like a million-billion-zillion! But here's the trick. No matter what number you think of, add one to it. No matter how high we may count, there's always one more number! Numbers go on forever!

David wrote in the Psalms that God's love lasts forever. Forever is another way of saying, no matter how many days you may think of, with God there is always one more day. God's love lasts forever. It never runs out! There's plenty for you and me! So how long will God love you? That's right! Forever and a day!

Word Watch

Give thanks to the LORD, for he is good. His love endures forever.

Psalm 136:1

~

God's **love** is never **ending**

MY PRAYER FOR TODAY

Lord, what a mighty love we find in You. It is a love that has no end. Thank You for such a great love! Amen.

Three Times a Day

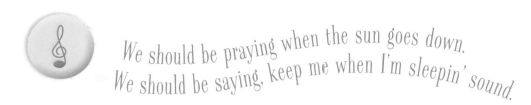

We should be praying when the sun goes down.
We should be saying, keep me when I'm sleepin' sound.

The fire alarm was ringing, but no one panicked. We knew what to do. We had practiced the fire drill many times before. Down the hallway we went, then out the door onto the soccer field. We were safe!

Daniel had a drill he practiced every day. I call it the "kneel drill." Daniel would kneel down and talk to God three times a day. When Daniel was cast into a lions' den, he didn't panic. He had practiced his "kneel drill." He knew God was able to save. He knew God was there with him. Do you pray every day? Let's be like Daniel. Practice your "kneel drill" and pray every day!

Word Watch

The prayer of a righteous man is powerful and effective.

James 5:16

Pray **every** day

MY PRAYER FOR TODAY

Lord, teach me to pray without ceasing. Amen.

The Golden Rule

It's simple as can be; it's good for you and me.
It teaches us to be better boys and girls, you see.

Jesus taught us to treat others the way we want to be treated. We call this Bible verse "the golden rule." It's golden because, like gold, it is rare to see and it has great value. If everyone practiced this rule, people all over the world would learn to be patient and kind to one another. Don't listen to those who say, "Do to others *before* they do it to you." Or, "Do the *same thing* to others that they do to you."

Do you want to be listened to? Then listen! Do you want people to share with you? Then share! Do you think you can do it? I know you can! Be golden and practice "the golden rule."

Word Watch

Do to others what you would have them do to you.

Matthew 7:12

THE GOLDEN RULE
CD 1
SONG 46

Do
unto
others

MY PRAYER FOR TODAY

Lord, may I always treat people
the way I want to be treated. Amen.

99

Jonah's Song

Call upon the Lord in your trouble.
Call upon the Lord and you will be saved today.

There's an important phone number you need to use only in an emergency. That number is 9-1-1. Tell the person who answers about the trouble. He or she will take care of everything. It is very wise to know whom to call in case of an emergency.

Jonah was sinking deep below the ocean waves. He was in big trouble! He needed God's help! Inside the belly of a giant fish, Jonah made the call. No—not a phone call; he called to the Lord! Once Jonah's call was made, God took care of everything. Jonah was saved because he called! He called upon the Lord! Whom do you call when you are in trouble? Call on the Lord!

Word Watch

In my distress I called to the LORD, and he answered me.

Jonah 2:2

Call on the **name** of the **Lord**

MY PRAYER FOR TODAY

Lord, when I am in trouble, teach me
to call on Your name. Amen.

Stand Up, Stand Up for Jesus

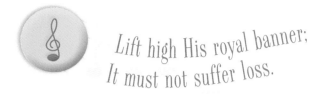

*Lift high His royal banner;
It must not suffer loss.*

In this hymn, we sing about Christians as soldiers. It speaks of an enemy who is real, and a battle between good and evil. Good people seek to please God. Evil people do what pleases themselves.

At work, Mom and Dad stand up for Jesus by doing what is right. At school, you can stand up for Jesus by being kind to a new student, or inviting someone to church. Doing this helps Christians win the victory. What does victory look like? Children coming to Christ, families staying together, nations turning back to God—that's what victory looks like. Christian soldiers, stand up for Jesus!

Word Watch

Therefore put on the full armor of God, so that when the
day of evil comes, you may be able to stand your ground,
and after you have done everything, to stand.

Ephesians 6:13

STAND UP, STAND UP FOR JESUS

CD 1
SONG 48

Do what is **right**

MY PRAYER FOR TODAY

Lord, help me to stand up for Jesus everywhere I go. Amen.

God Is Great

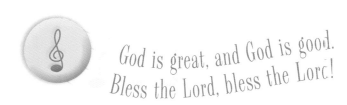

God is great, and God is good.
Bless the Lord, bless the Lord!

We take so many things for granted! We turn a faucet and out comes clean water. Yet there are places on Earth where there is no water at all. We flip a switch and on come the lights. Yet half of the world is without electricity. And when mealtime comes, we go to the grocery store to buy any kind of food we want. Yet there are places throughout the world today where food is in short supply.

With water, food, and light in such abundance, do we ever stop to say thank You? Maybe this is a good time to thank God for all He has given us. Let us say together, "Lord, we thank You for all You have given us. God, You are great. God, You are so good!"

Word Watch

Great is the LORD, and most worthy of praise.

Psalm 48:1

GOD IS GREAT
CD 1
SONG 49

~

Father,
we
thank
You

MY PRAYER FOR TODAY

Lord, You are great and worthy of my praise.
Thank You for supplying our food each day. Amen.

Leaning on the Everlasting Arms

 I have blessed peace with my Lord so near,
Leaning on the everlasting arms.

After working hard one day, I stopped to rest and leaned up against a wall. At least I thought it was a wall. But it was just a pile of rocks. As it starting moving, I started falling! I learned a lesson that day. If you're going to lean on something, you better be sure that it's strong enough to keep you from falling.

The Bible teaches us to lean on God. In good times or bad, He is the one who holds us up. He is able to keep us from falling. Do you need a friend to lean on? Lean on God. He is a strong tower, a Rock, and He never moves!

Word Watch

Listen! The LORD's arm is not too weak to save you.

Isaiah 59:1 NLT

The
Lord
is
my
Rock

MY PRAYER FOR TODAY

Lord, when my troubles are many, when my troubles are few, help me remember to lean on You. Amen.

All Night, All Day

Sleep, my child, and take your rest,
Angels watchin' over me.

Angels are heavenly messengers sent by God. An angel named Gabriel was sent to tell Mary about the birth of Jesus. Daniel told us of an angel sent by God to save him from the lions. An angel encouraged Gideon by saying, "God is with you." Peter was in prison, bound by chains, when an angel appeared, and the chains fell off.

The Bible says that God commands the angels to guard you in all your ways. One thing we know for sure: they are always sent by God to protect and comfort. As you sleep tonight, God's angels will watch over you!

Word Watch

For he will command his angels concerning you
to guard you in all your ways.

Psalm 91:11

~

Angels
will
watch
over
you

MY PRAYER FOR TODAY

Lord, thank You for taking care of me.
Angels are just another sign of Your love. Amen.

He's Got the Whole World in His Hands

He's got you and me, brother, in His hands.
He's got the whole world in His hands.

Isaiah wrote that God measured the waters that fill the ocean in the hollow of His hand. And with His hand, He marked off how big the heavens would be. What a mighty God! David looked up at a million stars and said the skies were the work of God's hands. Who can do what the hands of our God have done? Nobody!

In His hands we are safe and secure. In His hands we find love and comfort. We can rest in the same hands that quiet the wind and calm the raging sea. Whose hands are we talking about? God's hands! He's got the whole world in His hands. Let's clap our hands for Him!

Word Watch

The heavens declare the glory of God;

the skies proclaim the work of his hands.

Psalm 19:1

What
a
mighty
God
we
serve

MY PRAYER FOR TODAY

Father, I rest, knowing the whole
world is in Your hands. Amen.

Go, Tell It on the Mountain

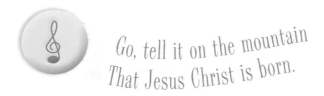

*Go, tell it on the mountain
That Jesus Christ is born.*

My brother entered a coloring contest sponsored by a local bakery. He was proud of the picture he had drawn of our family at the dinner table, eating bread. When it was announced that he won first prize, we couldn't wait to tell everyone the good news!

When something special happens, you want to tell everyone! Well, something special has happened! And that something special has a name. His name is Jesus. God so loved the world that He sent His Son to be born in a stable in Bethlehem. His name means "God saves." And that's the good news we must tell . . . Jesus has come to save! Are you saved? How do you know? You love and trust in Jesus!

Word Watch

For God so loved the world that he gave his one and only Son.

John 3:16

Jesus
Christ
is
born

MY PRAYER FOR TODAY

Father, something special has happened to me. I am saved!
I will tell everyone about Jesus' love! Amen.

This Is My Father's World

This is my Father's world, the birds their carols raise,
The morning light, the lily white, declare their Maker's praise.

If you were to open up a clock, you would see the hundreds of moving parts. Its design is very complicated. Yet look around! This world is much more complicated than a clock!

This song says that the "rocks and trees, the skies and seas; *His* hand these wonders wrought." That means God designed and made them. All this beauty didn't just happen—it was wrought. It was designed and made by my heavenly Father. This is *my* Father's world. Is He your Father too? If not, He can be! Then the wonder of salvation will be wrought in you!

Word Watch

And what is the exceeding greatness of his power . . .
which he wrought in Christ, when he raised him from the dead.
Ephesians 1:19-20 KJV

The
heavens
declare
God's
glory

MY PRAYER FOR TODAY

Father, all that I see . . . the earth, the skies,
and seas were wrought by You. Amen.

Jesus Loves Me

Jesus loves me! This I know,
For the Bible tells me so.

Without a doubt, Jesus loves you and me. How can I be so sure? Because the Bible tells me so! The Bible is a very special book. In it, we read the very words of God. It tells the wonderful story of Jesus and His love for you and me. Here's what Jesus said: "As the Father has loved me, so have I loved you" (John 15:9).

How much did Jesus love you and me? It can't be measured in hugs and kisses. It was measured in the life He gave. He loved us so much that He stretched His arms wide open . . . not to give a hug, but to die on a cross. Think of someone you can tell about the love of Jesus today!

Word Watch

There is no greater love than to lay down one's life for one's friends.

John 15:13 NLT

116

~
Share
the
love
of
Jesus

MY PRAYER FOR TODAY

Lord, help me share the love
of Jesus with everyone. Amen.

Think About These Things

Oh, what should we think about?
Things so great, found in Philippians 4:8.

It's nice to find a shady spot sometimes and think about all the good things in this world. What things do you think about?

The Bible says that we should think about things that are *true*. It's true that Jesus loves me. So I'll think about Jesus. It also says that we should think about things that are *noble*. To be noble is to have a good character, like when we show kindness. I can think about being kind to someone today. Finally, we should think about things that are *right*. It's right to praise God. I think I'll praise Him right now for this beautiful day! Now what do you want to think about?

Word Watch

Finally, brothers, whatever is true, whatever is noble,

whatever is right . . . think about such things.

Philippians 4:8

~

Fill
your
mind
with
God's
Word

MY PRAYER FOR TODAY

Father, You have created my brain to be filled with good things. May I always think of You. Amen.

119

Jesus Loves the Little Children

Red and yellow, black and white, they are precious in His sight. Jesus loves the little children of the world!

It's important to know that Jesus loves everyone, not just you and me! He loves your friends at school and your neighbors across the street. His love doesn't stop there! He even loves those who speak a different language, halfway around the world. The color of their skin doesn't matter. Where they come from doesn't matter. God made all people, everywhere, and He loves each one. They are all precious to His Son, Jesus.

Things that are precious have great value to the owner . . . like a diamond ring. You are loved by God. You are precious to Him. Do you feel precious? You are! You're more precious than diamonds to our God above!

Word Watch

How precious are your thoughts about me,

O God. They cannot be numbered!

Psalm 139:17 NLT

You
are
precious
to
Jesus

MY PRAYER FOR TODAY

Father, You are precious to me.
I know I am precious to You. Amen.

I Have Decided to Follow Jesus

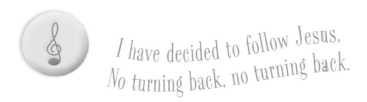

*I have decided to follow Jesus,
No turning back, no turning back.*

It was a bad storm! But someone was out there walking in the pouring rain. It was the mailman! Then I remembered his motto: "Neither snow, nor rain, nor gloom of night keeps me from my appointed rounds." Now, that's commitment! *Commitment* is a promise to do what you say you will do!

Commitment to a job is a good thing. But commitment to Jesus is a *great* thing. When you decide to follow Jesus, you promise to do the things He would do. Sometimes it's easy. Sometimes it's not so easy. That's because we have to learn to share and be kind to others—even when they are not kind to us. Have you decided to follow Jesus? Then make a commitment to do the things He would do!

Word Watch

Choose for yourselves this day whom you will serve.

Joshua 24:15

Choose
to
follow
Jesus

MY PRAYER FOR TODAY

Father, I will choose to serve You. Amen.

For the Beauty of the Earth

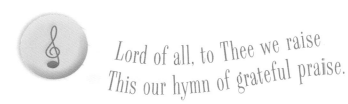

Lord of all, to Thee we raise
This our hymn of grateful praise.

See the butterfly resting on the little girl's finger? God made that butterfly, and God made little girls too! In fact, God made everything in this big, beautiful world. For that, we give Him praise. To give praise means that we give God credit for all He has done.

Have you ever given praise to God for His creation? It's easy to do! Just say, "Thank You, Lord, for all You have made. And thank You, Lord, for making me!" There . . . you did it! You have given praise to the Lord! You can even sing praise to the One who created the beauty of the earth!

Word Watch

I am the LORD, who has made all things, who alone
stretched out the heavens, who spread out the earth by myself.

Isaiah 44:24

~

God
made
all
things
beautiful

MY PRAYER FOR TODAY

Lord, I praise You for all You have done.
You alone have made all things. Amen.

The Lord's Prayer

*For Yours is the kingdom and the power
And the glory, forever and ever.*

The people gathered on a mountainside to hear Jesus teach. They wanted to know how to pray. Jesus taught them the Lord's Prayer (Matthew 6:9–13):

Our Father in heaven,
He first taught them who to pray to: the Father.
hallowed be your name,
God's name is to be held in honor above all others.
your kingdom come, your will be done on earth as it is in heaven.
We are to make God known and do what He asks.
Give us today our daily bread. Forgive us our debts as we also have forgiven our debtors.
Then we ask for the things we need; things like bread for our bodies and forgiveness.
And lead us not into temptation, but deliver us from the evil one.
Ask Him to guide us to do good things.

Jesus finished by teaching us to close our prayer with praise! Praise God for who He is. Trust God for what tomorrow may bring.

Our Father in heaven, hallowed be your name.

Matthew 6:9

Praise
God
for
who
He
is

MY PRAYER FOR TODAY

Father, I want to pray the way Jesus taught.
So I pray to You, and I praise You for all that You do. Amen.

Do Your Best, Child

No matter what the job, always do your best,
Because someone will be watching, I am sure.

Their intentions were good. They got up early Saturday morning, just like Dad asked. They gathered paint cans and brushes. Off they went to paint the fence. Things were going well. Then everything turned upside down, including the paint cans! What happened?

The puppy next door knocked over the paint . . . what a mess! Dad came running. The boys explained that they had done their best. Dad chuckled, then gave them a hug and said, "God only expects our best. Then we leave the rest to Him." Everyone laughed!

Is there a job you need to do? Do your best. God will be pleased, even if it does get a little messy!

Word Watch

Do your best to present yourself to God as one approved, a workman who does not need to be ashamed and who correctly handles the word of truth.

2 Timothy 2:15

Work
as
if
for
God

MY PRAYER FOR TODAY

Father, help me do my best as I work for You. Amen.

Go Fish, Go Fish!

People need the Lord today.
So cast the gospel net their way, and go fish! Go fish!

Peter, James, and John were discouraged. They didn't know if they would ever see Jesus again. So they went back to the only thing they knew—fishing. They had been fishing all night, but they had caught no fish. Then a familiar voice said, "Throw your net on the right side of the boat." When they did, the nets were suddenly full of fish!

John said, "It's Jesus!" Peter was so excited, he jumped out of the boat and swam to shore. Jesus hadn't left them. He was there all the time! Sometimes we may feel as if Jesus is far away. But He has promised to never leave us. Don't trust your feelings; trust Him!

Never will I leave you; never will I forsake you.

Hebrews 13:5

Jesus
will
never
leave
you

MY PRAYER FOR TODAY

Father, I thank You for Your promise to never leave me. Amen.

Try to Be Kind

To each other, sister and brother,
To everyone, to everyone else, be kind.

Billy had been unusually quiet the last few days. His dad was in the Navy and was far away, serving our country. Susie noticed and prayed with her mom, "Lord, what can we do to show kindness to Billy?" Then an answer came! She would have a pool party and invite all her friends, including Billy.

Billy arrived and sat quietly until Susie spoke. "Billy, everyone is so proud of you and your daddy. We wanted to show you in some small way. This is for you!" She handed Billy a very special gift. It was a sailboat that said *US Navy* on the side! The kindness she had shown made Billy so happy! Is there someone you know who needs a little kindness? Show it today!

Word Watch

Always try to be kind to each other and to everyone else.

I Thessalonians 5:15

Kindness
heals
a
hurting
heart

MY PRAYER FOR TODAY

Father, help me to have eyes to see those in
need of a little kindness. Amen.

O, How I Love Jesus

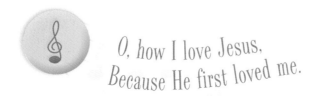

O, how I love Jesus,
Because He first loved me.

Jesus was teaching inside a small house. Hundreds of people were waiting to get inside. They were crowded in the doorways and sitting in the windows. Some men arrived carrying a sick friend on a stretcher. They loved Jesus and knew He could heal their friend. But the crowds were so big, they couldn't get near. They didn't give up, though!

They went up onto the roof. They made a hole big enough to lower their friend down, right in front of Jesus. These friends wouldn't let anything stop them from seeing Jesus! What can we do to help a friend see Jesus? We can invite our friend to church. Jesus healed the sick man because his friends wouldn't give up. Friends help friends see Jesus!

Word Watch

We love him, because he first loved us.

1 John 4:19 KJV

Friends
help
friends
see
Jesus

MY PRAYER FOR TODAY

Father, I love You. Thank You for loving us
by sending Your Son, Jesus. Amen.

Even the Wind Obeys

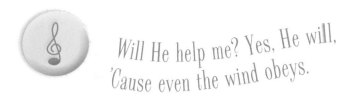

*Will He help me? Yes, He will,
'Cause even the wind obeys.*

Jesus drifted to sleep in the boat as His disciples sailed across the lake. Suddenly, a terrible storm began to rock the boat. But Jesus didn't wake up. The disciples were afraid. "Teacher!" they shouted. "Don't You know we could drown?"

Jesus faced the wind and shouted, "Quiet! Be still!" Immediately the wind stopped and the waves were still. He turned and said, "Why were you so frightened? Where is your faith?"

That's a question we still ask ourselves. When things go wrong and we are afraid, where is our faith? God is bigger than any storm. But we must believe! Jesus said that our Father knows what we need before we ask. So have faith! If He can calm the stormy waves, He can calm the storm in you.

Word Watch

Even the wind and the waves obey him!

Mark 4:41

~
God
is
in
control

MY PRAYER FOR TODAY

Father, I believe that You are in control of all things;
not just the wind and waves, but the things that worry me. Amen.

Rainbows

A promise I make to you, here's why—never again will waters rise, for I have set My rainbow in the sky.

Road signs are very helpful. They give us good information as we travel down the road. But there's another kind of sign God put way up in the sky. Have you seen it? It's called a rainbow!

God put a rainbow in the sky after Noah's flood. He said it was a sign of His promise. What was the promise? Never again will floodwaters cover the earth. So the next time you see a rainbow, remember these two things: there is a loving God who promises to save us, and He is faithful to keep that promise!

Word Watch

I have set my rainbow in the clouds, and it will be the sign
of the promise between me and the earth.

Genesis 9:13

~

God
always
keeps
His
promises

MY PRAYER FOR TODAY

Father, I will trust in Your promise. Amen.

Jesus Loves Even Me

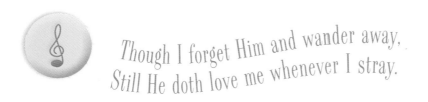

Though I forget Him and wander away,
Still He doth love me whenever I stray.

People gathered around to listen to Jesus teach. Suddenly, a woman accused of doing bad things was pushed down in front of Him. Angry men with stones shouted, "Moses said to stone such a person. What do You say?"

Jesus looked up and said, "You who have never sinned, cast the first stone." No one threw a stone. They knew they had all sinned too. No one is perfect, only Jesus!

We must never judge others. We have all done bad things. Jesus said, "For in the same way you judge others, you will be judged" (Matthew 7:2). What should we do instead? Forgive! Her accusers walked away. Jesus told her to go and do good things. Jesus loved her, and He loves you too!

Word Watch

Do not judge, or you too will be judged.

Matthew 7:1

~

The **love** of **Jesus** is **perfect**

MY PRAYER FOR TODAY

Father, may I always forgive and never judge.
For only Jesus is perfect. Amen.

The Kingdom of Heaven

*Where your treasure is,
There your heart will be also.*

Parables are little stories that teach big lessons. Jesus told this parable about heaven: "The kingdom of heaven is like a merchant looking for pearls. The merchant finds a very valuable pearl. He desires to have this pearl so much, he sells all that he has and buys the beautiful pearl." Now, what do pearls have to do with heaven?

The merchant in the story is Jesus Himself. The pearl He finds is you, and all those who love Jesus. The story says a great price was paid by the merchant (Jesus) to buy these pearls. What price did Jesus pay? He paid with His life on the cross. Imagine, Jesus thinks of you as a pearl! He left His heavenly home because He loved you, His treasured pearl!

Word Watch

The kingdom of heaven is like a merchant looking for fine pearls.

Matthew 13:45

You **are** a **treasured** pearl

MY PRAYER FOR TODAY

Father, I thank You for Jesus. He left His heavenly home to search for me, as for a precious pearl. Amen.

143

Little children, Obey

Obey God's Word today,
For this pleases Jesus.

Mom made a list of chores she wanted me to do. Wash the dog, water the lawn, and take out the trash . . . easy enough! But then along came a couple of my friends. "Come on," they said. "You can do all that stuff later. Let's go swimming!" I had a choice to make.

What would you do? Remember, who we become when we grow up depends on the choices we make now. We must learn to obey our parents first. Then, as we grow up, we obey God. I said to the guys, "I'll meet you when I've finished these chores Mom gave me to do." To obey is the best choice. It pleases the Lord!

Word Watch

Children, obey your parents in everything, for this pleases the Lord.

Colossians 3:20

~

To
obey
is
the
best
choice

MY PRAYER FOR TODAY

Father, help me make good choices.
Good choices begin with obeying my parents. Amen.

I Will Make You Fishers of Men

*I will make you fishers of men,
If you follow Me.*

Jesus told Peter he would become a "fisher of men." What does that mean? First, a fisherman has to attract the fish; so he must know the fish's habits and ways. That's how he gets them hooked; then he pulls the fish out of the water. Fishers of men must know the habits and ways of people. They attract people by telling them about Jesus; then they pull men out of the world.

A fisherman has to go where the fish are. They won't come to you! Likewise, fishers of men are commanded by Jesus to go where the people are. He said, "Go into all the world and preach the good news" (Mark 16:15). That could be across the street or around the world. Have you ever been fishing for Jesus? Be a fisher of men!

I
must
know,
go,
and
tell

Word Watch

"Come follow me," Jesus said, "and I will
make you fishers of men."

Matthew 4:19

MY PRAYER FOR TODAY

Father, I want to be a fisher of men.
Help me to know, go, and tell. Amen.

147

Trust and Obey

For there's no other way
To be happy in Jesus, but to trust and obey.

We were boarding the plane to fly to the island of St. Croix. As we boarded, the pilot said with confidence, "Fasten your seat belt." We did what he said. Then he started up the engines. We trusted him to fly us safely to St. Croix.

Jesus wants us to trust and obey Him like the lame man at the Pool of Bethesda did. He had been lying there for thirty-eight years. Jesus had compassion and asked him, "Do you want to get well? Get up and walk!" The man trusted Jesus and obeyed. He stood up and walked! Let's all trust and obey Jesus every day.

Word Watch

O LORD my God, in You I put my trust.

Psalm 7:1 NKJV

~
God
is
able

MY PRAYER FOR TODAY

Father, I will rest in the mighty power of Jesus Christ. He is able to do all things. Amen.

Now the Day Is Over

With Thy tender blessing
May our eyelids close.

At the end of every busy day, we all need to rest. We brush our teeth, hop into bed, and snuggle up under the covers. But before we close our eyelids tight, there's something we should always remember. Do you know what it is?

We should pray. Yes, the day may be over, but tomorrow will be here soon. Bedtime prayer is the time we thank God for today and give Him our tomorrow. When Mom and Dad pray with you, it's even better! When does sleepy time begin? Let it begin when prayer time ends!

Word Watch

I will lie down and sleep in peace, for you alone,

O Lord, make me dwell in safety.

Psalm 4:8

Give
God
your
tomorrow

MY PRAYER FOR TODAY

Lord, the day is over and I am ready to sleep.
May tomorrow be a good day! Amen.

151

The Loaves and Fishes Song

Five thousand were fed with five little loaves.
Five thousand were fed with two little fish.

People were seeking Jesus. A crowd of five thousand or more had gathered to hear Him teach about God's kingdom. Lunchtime came, and all the people were hungry. But they had no food. What would they do? A little boy gave his lunch to Jesus—but how could five little loaves of bread and two small fish feed this crowd?

Small meals become great miracles when blessed by Jesus. He looked up to heaven and blessed the small lunch. Then it was given to the big crowd. Everyone ate, and there were still twelve baskets of food left over! This mealtime miracle shows that God provides for those who seek Him.

Word Watch

Taking the five loaves and the two fish
and looking up to heaven, he gave thanks.
Mark 6:41

~

God
will
provide

MY PRAYER FOR TODAY

Father, those who seek You are blessed.
May I be willing to give my all to You. Amen.

Footprints on the Water

I saw Jesus, Jesus, walking on the waves—
Footprints on the water that day.

The disciples sailed across the lake while Jesus stayed behind to pray. The wind began to blow so hard, they could hardly row their boat. Jesus saw their trouble. He wouldn't let anything separate Him from the ones He loved. So Jesus went out to them. No, He didn't swim . . . and He didn't row a boat. He walked on the water! It was a miracle!

Peter saw Jesus coming. He stepped out of the boat and began to walk to Jesus. But he took his eyes off Jesus and began to watch the waves. He started to sink. Jesus reached out and saved him. "Why did you doubt?" Jesus asked.

Have you ever doubted Jesus? Don't sink down into worry and trouble. Keep your eyes on Jesus and walk by faith, wherever He goes!

Word Watch

Take courage! It is I. Don't be afraid.

Mark 6:50

Let
us
walk
by
faith

MY PRAYER FOR TODAY

Father, teach me to walk by faith, even if
it leads me out on the water. Amen.

We're Going to God's House Today

I rejoice with those who say to me,
"Let us go to the house of the Lord."

My brother and I were moping around the house on a rainy afternoon. Dad knew we needed a lift. He asked, "Would anyone like to go with me to the Game House?" Would we ever! The Game House had lots of video games and fun things to do. We could talk, meet friends, and share the fun!

Going to church should be like that! It's a place where people come together to talk, meet friends, and share what God is doing in their lives. We hear stories of God's miracles and mercy. We come to pray and encourage each other. You can have a good time at the Game House. But you can have a *great* time at God's house. I can't wait to go to church! Can you?

Word Watch

Let us not give up meeting together, as some are in the habit of doing.

Hebrews 10:25

Rejoice
with
the
family
of
God

MY PRAYER FOR TODAY

Father, may I rejoice with other believers
as I go to church. Amen.

157

The Mustard Seed Song

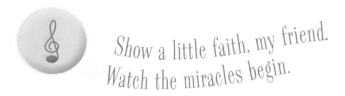

Show a little faith, my friend.
Watch the miracles begin.

They were building a highway, and a mountain was standing in the way. It took a hundred days to move that mountain. Giant steam shovels and dump trucks worked night and day. At last the road was completed. A huge mountain had been moved by men and machines!

Jesus talked about moving mountains. He compared faith to a mustard seed. Mustard seeds are very tiny. But Jesus taught that a little faith can move big mountains. That's because our faith is in a God bigger than any mountain. Mustard seeds grow into large bushes. Our faith can grow bigger too! If there is something that seems impossible in your life, have a little faith in our great big God. He can move impossible mountains!

Word Watch

I tell you the truth, if you have faith as small as a mustard seed,

you can say to this mountain, "Move from here to there,"

and it will move. Nothing will be impossible for you.

Matthew 17:20

The
Lord
can
move
mountains

MY PRAYER FOR TODAY

Father, I pray that my faith will grow
like the mustard seed into a great big tree! Amen.

159

The Plans I Have for You

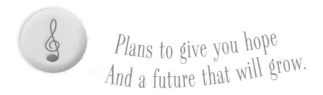

*Plans to give you hope
And a future that will grow.*

Mom hired a designer to help her remodel her kitchen. The designer opened up the plans she had drawn and spread them out on the kitchen table. The work took six weeks to complete. Lots of hammers and nails! But the kitchen looked great, thanks to the designer's plan.

God is like a designer. He has a plan for your life. His plan will not harm you, so you don't have to be afraid. It's something He created you to do. Only God knows what He has planned for you. But you'll find out as you get older. Ever wonder what you'll be when you grow up? Seek the Lord, and you'll find God's wonderful plan for you!

Word Watch

*For we are . . . created in Christ Jesus to do good works,
which God prepared in advance for us to do.*

Ephesians 2:10

God has a **plan** for you

MY PRAYER FOR TODAY

Father, I believe that You have a plan for my life.
Help me seek You always. Amen.

Be Thou My Vision

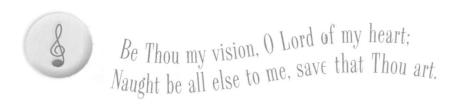

Be Thou my vision, O Lord of my heart;
Naught be all else to me, save that Thou art.

Once, Jesus met a blind man. It was very unusual, but He put mud on the man's eyes. Then He told him to go wash. The blind man did what Jesus said. As he cleared away the mud, he could see for the very first time!

This old hymn has become our prayer. We ask to see the world as Jesus sees it. Let us see the hurting. Help us to love them the way Jesus would. May He give us wisdom and guide every thought. Help us to think like Jesus. And when we speak, may we speak with the love of Jesus. Isn't this a wonderful prayer song? "Be Thou my vision," Jesus.

Word Watch

Open my eyes that I may see wonderful things in your law.

Psalm 119:18

~

Share
Jesus
with
those
in
need

MY PRAYER FOR TODAY

Father, give me eyes to see a world of need around me.
And may I share as Jesus would. Amen.

Love Your Neighbor as Yourself

We gotta share the love of Jesus,
Share it with everyone.

Jesus was asked a tricky question, "If we are to love our neighbor as ourselves, who then is my neighbor?" Jesus answered the question with a story. He told of a man who was beaten by robbers and left by the road to die. Three men came by, but only one stopped to help. Jesus asked, "Which of the three men was a good neighbor?"

"The one who helped!"

Jesus said, "Then go and do likewise." That's what a good neighbor does. He will go and show love and compassion to those he meets. Do you want to be a good neighbor? Then go and show the love of Jesus to all!

Word Watch

Jesus told him, "Go and do likewise."

Luke 10:37

Show
the
love
of
Jesus
to
all

MY PRAYER FOR TODAY

Father, I want to be a good neighbor. Help me
"go and show" the love of Jesus to all. Amen.

The Lord Is My Shepherd

The Lord is like a shepherd; He knows what to do.
When His little lambs are tired, He'll help them through!

A shepherd is a person who cares for sheep. He has three important jobs: First, he leads the sheep. A shepherd must lead his sheep to a safe haven. Second, he feeds the sheep. He takes them to grassy meadows where the sheep can rest and be fed. And last, a shepherd meets the needs of his sheep. If one little lamb gets hurt or lost, he goes and finds him.

Our Lord is like a shepherd. He leads us in the right way, He feeds us our daily bread, and He supplies all our needs. That is why I say, "The Lord is my shepherd!" Is He your shepherd too? He leads, He feeds, and He meets your needs!

The LORD is my shepherd, I shall not be in want.

Psalm 23:1

THE LORD IS MY SHEPHERD
CD 2
SONG 30

The
**Lord
leads**
me
and
feeds
me

MY PRAYER FOR TODAY

Father, thank You for being my shepherd who leads me, feeds me, and supplies my needs. Amen.

Song of the Prodigal Son

Jesus told a story of a young man who decided to leave home. His father gave him money. The young man went away and quickly spent all he had doing bad things. He had no money to buy food. One day, he was so hungry, he thought, *Maybe my father will let me be a servant. I'll go home.*

When he got there, his father ran to meet him. He even gave him presents! The older brother said, "It's not fair!" Neither brother understood a father's love. A father's love forgives! The same is true with our heavenly Father. When you do bad things, do you think God forgives you? Yes, He does! His love is bigger than any sin.

Who is a God like you, who
pardons sin and forgives?

Micah 7:18

The
Lord
forgives
me

MY PRAYER FOR TODAY

Father, thank You for forgiving me when I do wrong.
May I always run to You for forgiveness. Amen.

169

Deep and Wide

There's a fountain flowing deep and wide.

I love the ocean! It reminds me of this song. It tells me that God's love is deep and wide! The word *deep* used in the Bible is *bathos*, which means "extreme."

God has shown you and me extreme love. How deep and wide it is! He went to great lengths to show how much He loved us. How extreme was God's love? For God so loved the world that He sent His only Son. Jesus gave His life for us. Now, that's extreme love! How deep is your love for God? Let it be deep and wide!

Word Watch

I pray that you … may have power … to grasp how wide
and long and high and deep is the love of Christ.

Ephesians 3:17-18

DEEP AND WIDE

CD 2

SONG 32

Who can **measure** God's **love?**

MY PRAYER FOR TODAY

Father, Your love is so deep and wide, no one can even measure it! Thank You for Your love. Amen.

Zacchaeus Was a Wee Little Man

"Zacchaeus, you come down from there,
For I'm going to your house today."

When Jesus saw Zacchaeus up in the tree, He said, "Zacchaeus, come down. I am going to stay at your house today!" I'll bet Zacchaeus was surprised! If Jesus were coming to your house today, would you have to make any changes?

Would you have to change the channel on the TV? Would you have to throw away some of your magazines? What about your Bible—would you have to find it and dust it off? What about your heart? Any changes needed? Zacchaeus's heart was changed when Jesus came to visit. He was saved! Let's live every day as though Jesus were coming to visit!

Word Watch

[Jesus] looked up and said to him, "Zacchaeus,
come down immediately. I must stay at your house today."

Luke 19:5

Live
like
Jesus
is
coming
today

MY PRAYER FOR TODAY

Father, help me live as though Jesus is coming to my house today. Amen.

173

Sharing Is caring

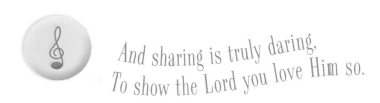

And sharing is truly daring,
To show the Lord you love Him so.

Mom only had one bottle of Big Bubbles. So Brian and Anna would have to share. Brian blew bubbles while Anna chased after them. Then Anna blew bubbles. *Pop! Pop! Pop!* As she watched from the doorway, Mom was pleased. They were sharing! And sharing is what Jesus would do!

The Bible tells the story of two friends named Jonathan and David. They shared many things, including their bows and their swords (1 Samuel 18:4). A couple shared their home with the prophet Elijah and made a small room for him to stay in (2 Kings 4:8–10). Sharing the things we have is a good thing. It doesn't just please Mom; it pleases God!

Word Watch

Share with God's people who are in need.

Romans 12:13

Sharing
pleases
the
Lord

MY PRAYER FOR TODAY

Father, I know sharing is really caring for others.
May I care more and share more. Amen.

Hosanna

Hosanna, hosanna, hosanna to the King!

As Jesus came to Jerusalem, the crowd greeted Him by waving palm branches. They shouted, "Hosanna!" which means "Save us!" They believed Jesus was their Savior. He was sent by God to forgive the bad things they had done. So they welcomed their Savior and King! Their future belonged to Jesus. They would obey and follow wherever He led.

Is Jesus your Savior? Are your sins forgiven? Is He Lord of your life? Is your future in His hands? Make Jesus your Lord and Savior. Say, "I believe in You, Jesus. You are the King of kings, and Lord of lords; the One sent by God to save us. Hosanna to the King!"

Word Watch

Hosanna! Blessed is he who comes in the name of the Lord!

Mark 11:9

HOSANNA
CD 2
SONG 35

Bless
the
name
of
Jesus

MY PRAYER FOR TODAY

Father, may I always bless the name of Jesus.
He is my Lord. He is my Savior. Amen.

God Sees the Heart

Don't favor one if her eyes are blue;
God only sees the heart.

Jesus saw a rich man come into the temple. He knew the man was rich because his clothes were nice, and he carried a big bag of money. Jesus also saw a poor woman dressed in rags. She had only a few coins to give. Do you think Jesus showed special kindness to the rich man? Did He ignore the poor woman? Of course not!

Favoritism is when we treat one person with greater kindness than another. James said that we should never show favoritism. Why? Because *all* men and women, *all* boys and girls, are loved by God. We should treat them with the same kindness, regardless of what kind of clothes they wear or how much money they have. Can you show God's love to *all* boys and girls? God will be pleased!

Don't show favoritism.

James 2:1

~

Treat
people
with
kindness
and
respect

MY PRAYER FOR TODAY

Father, You are the God who created all people.
Help me to treat all people with kindness and respect. Amen.

179

Imitators of Jesus

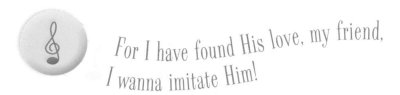

For I have found His love, my friend,
I wanna imitate Him!

I once saw a man who did an imitation of the president. He was dressed to look like him and he spoke just like him. His expressions and movements were those of the president. It was a perfect imitation. How did he learn to imitate the president so well? He had to watch the president and practice being like him.

The Bible says we are to imitate Jesus. We should try to do and say the things He did. What are those things? I can think of three important ones: Jesus loved, so we must imitate His love toward others. Jesus served, so we must imitate Him by serving others. Jesus obeyed, so we must imitate Jesus by obeying God's Word. Jesus loved, served, and obeyed. Let's be like Jesus!

Word Watch

[Jesus said,] "I have given you an example to follow.

Do as I have done to you."

John 13:15 NLT

~

Jesus **loved**, **served**, and **obeyed**

MY PRAYER FOR TODAY

Father, teach me to imitate Jesus, who loved, who served, and who obeyed. Amen.

Do Remember

 Do remember, remember what God has done.

Jesus and His disciples met to celebrate the Passover. He took the bread and broke it, saying, "This is My body broken for you." Then taking the cup He said, "This is My blood spilled out for you." Why did He do this? It was a great show-and-tell lesson.

Jesus said, "Do this to remember Me." Never forget the price Jesus paid for your forgiveness. Remember Him and the lessons He taught. Remember the miracles He performed. Never forget the power of God working through Him (Acts 2:22). Why do we have communion? To help us remember; we remember Jesus. We obey Jesus. We love Jesus!

Word Watch

This is my body given for you; do this in remembrance of me.

Luke 22:19

Jesus died for **you** and **me**

MY PRAYER FOR TODAY

Father, I obey the command of Jesus to break bread and take the cup in remembrance of His great sacrifice for me. Amen.

I Am Growing

*I am growing, I am growing,
Big and tall, big and tall. Growing up for Jesus!*

So you made a little mess. Well, actually . . . a big mess. But that's okay! Mom is patient. She knows that we learn by doing. And we need to learn to do things for ourselves as we grow. Did you know that the Bible says that Jesus grew?

How did He grow? The Bible says He grew in wisdom and stature and in favor with God and men. We all grow the very same way: Our minds grow and we learn new things; that's wisdom. Our bodies grow and we get taller and stronger; that's stature. Most importantly, our love for God and other people grows. What are the ways we grow? We grow in wisdom, in our stature, and in our love for God and others! I am growing big and tall for Jesus!

Word Watch

Jesus grew in wisdom, and stature, and in favor with God and men.

Luke 2:52

Grow **big** and **strong** for Jesus

MY PRAYER FOR TODAY

Father, as my mind and body grow, help my love to grow big and strong for Jesus. Amen.

The Old Rugged Cross

I will cling to the old rugged cross,
And exchange it someday for a crown.

When runners compete for a prize, they train very hard. What's at stake? A crown is given to the winner. A crown is a symbol of victory. It says you won the race. A crown is a symbol for Christians too. It's a symbol that we are winners. But this crown isn't won by you or me. It was won by Jesus and given to us.

Jesus won that great victory. People thought He was defeated when He died on the cross. But when He rose again, He proved He was the victor. Death was defeated. Because of the cross, we can win the prize of heaven! How do you get your crown? Just love Jesus with all your heart!

They do it to get a crown that will not last; but we do it to get a crown that will last forever.

1 Corinthians 9:25

THE OLD RUGGED CROSS

CD 2

SONG 40

~

Love
Jesus
with
all
your
heart

MY PRAYER FOR TODAY

Father, we know that one day Jesus will return.
On that day I will praise Him for the crown I receive! Amen.

Christ the Lord Is Risen Today

Christ the Lord is risen today. Alleluia!

Three days after Jesus died on the cross, Mary went to the tomb where He was buried. When angels appeared, the guards watching the tomb were terrified. The angel said to Mary, "Do not be afraid. Jesus is not here anymore. He is alive again. He has risen!"

What do we say to a God who can do this? How do we praise Him enough for all He has done? We can say with the hymn writer, "Alleluia!" which means "Praise the name of God." And when our risen Lord comes again, what will you say? "Alleluia! Praise the name of our God!"

Word Watch

I know that you are looking for Jesus, who was crucified.

He is not here; he has risen, just as he said.

Matthew 28:5-6

~

Praise
the
name
of
God

MY PRAYER FOR TODAY

Alleluia! Father, I praise Your name for
all You have done for me! Amen.

EVery EYe Shall See

Every eye shall see
Every eye shall see him come

After Jesus rose from the dead, He stayed on this earth forty more days. But His work on this earth was ending. The cross was behind Him and heaven awaited.

He gathered His disciples one last time. Jesus asked them to tell everyone what they had seen and heard. Then He was taken up into heaven. As He rose up into the sky, two angels appeared and said, "This same Jesus will come back from heaven in the very same way you have seen Him go into heaven." But on that day, every eye will see Him coming (Revelation 1:7). Why is He coming back? He's coming for you and me!

This same Jesus, who has been taken from you into heaven, will come back in the same way you have seen him go into heaven.

Acts 1:11

EVERY EYE SHALL SEE
CD 2
SONG 42

~

Jesus
is
coming
soon

MY PRAYER FOR TODAY

Father, I know Jesus is coming again.
Let me get my life ready for His return. Amen.

In All Things

And we know that in all things,
God works for the good of those who love Him.

How can being put in a lions' den be a good thing? God used Daniel to show a king His power. How can being in the belly of a whale be a good thing? God used Jonah to save the people of Nineveh. Sometimes God allows us to be uncomfortable so that others can come to know Him. While we are there, we must trust the Lord, who says, "All things are working together for good."

Paul was in prison for preaching. That's bad, you might think. No, that's good! Paul wrote the book of Romans while he was there. It's good because, just like Daniel, and just like Jonah, God was using Paul to save His people. God wants to use you too! Having a bad day? So was Paul. But it will work out for good!

Word Watch

And we know that in all things God works for the good of those

who love him, who have been called according to his purpose.

Romans 8:28

God
works
for
good

MY PRAYER FOR TODAY

Father, You have made a promise. I believe You.
No matter what happens, I trust You are working for my good. Amen.

Silver and Gold Have I None

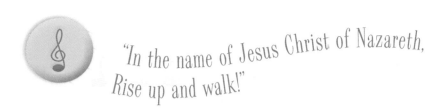

"In the name of Jesus Christ of Nazareth, Rise up and walk!"

Peter and John were going to church to pray. A man who could not walk called out to them, "Could you please give me some money?" Peter said, "I have something better than money to give you. In the name of Jesus, get up and walk!" Then he took him by the hand, and the man's legs and feet became strong.

Can you think of something money is good for? It can buy a ticket to Disney World, a shiny new bicycle, or a computer game. Money has a lot of spending power, but it has no Spirit power. Spending power can get you things here on the earth. But only Spirit power can get you the things of God. Would you like some Spirit power? You can't buy it with money! It's given by God through prayer.

Word Watch

Silver or gold I do not have, but what I have I give you.

Acts 3:6

~

Spirit
power
comes
by
prayer

MY PRAYER FOR TODAY

Father, money is a tool. If we use it for Your glory,
it is good. May I always glorify You. Amen.

Isn't He Wonderful?

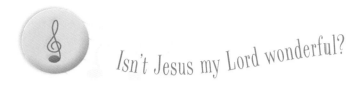

Isn't Jesus my Lord wonderful?

Jesus is wonderful. The prophet Isaiah even called him "Wonderful Counselor." What did he mean? A wonderful counselor is wise. He listens to your problems and helps you find an answer. Jesus is like that. He is always there to listen, and He always has an answer.

He's more than a wonderful counselor. He's a wonderful Savior and friend. And He's building a wonderful home for you in heaven that will last forever. And one day, the wonder of all wonders, our Lord Jesus will come again. And do you know why? Because He loves you! Why does Jesus love you so much? Because He is a wonderful Lord!

Word Watch

He showed his wonderful love to me.

Psalm 31:21

Thank You, **God**, for **loving** me

MY PRAYER FOR TODAY

Father, You are wonderful. Thank You for loving me, guiding me, and giving me a heavenly home. Amen.

197

Working for the Lord

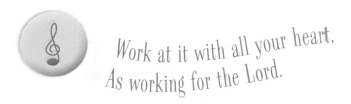

Work at it with all your heart,
As working for the Lord.

Jesus prayed to His heavenly Father, "I have brought you glory on earth by completing the work you gave me to do" (John 17:4). Jesus finished every job given to Him by the Father. Some were easier than others. But He did each one with *all* His heart.

God is working all the time to make you more like Jesus. So He gives us little jobs to do. Some jobs grow our patience; some test our faith. Maybe your job is to clean the dishes or sweep the floor. Whatever it is, remember: God is working out His plan through you. If He has given you a job, do it to the best of your ability. That pleases Him . . . and it gives Him glory!

Word Watch

Whatever you do, work at it with all your heart,

as working for the Lord, not for men.

Colossians 3:23

~

I **want** to be like **Jesus**

MY PRAYER FOR TODAY

Father, whatever job I may have, help me work
at it with all my heart so You are glorified. Amen.

The B-I-B-L-E

I stand alone on the Word of God,
The B-I-B-L-E!

There are books that tell us anything we want to know. But there is one book like no other. It's called the Bible. It's really a library of sixty-six books, written by thirty-seven different authors, all inspired by one God. It begins at the beginning of time, and it ends . . . at the end of time and the beginning of eternity.

In between, we read stories of great men of faith, like Moses and Abraham. We read about the miracles of a mighty God who loves and saves His people. You can't put this book down without making a choice. Do you believe it? Will you trust in the God who wrote it? Yes, I will! That's why the B-I-B-L-E is the book for me.

Word Watch

Your word is a lamp to my feet and a light for my path.

Psalm 119:105

Trust the **God** of the **Bible**

MY PRAYER FOR TODAY

Father, I know that if we stand for nothing, we may fall for anything. So I stand on the Bible alone. Amen.

Behold, Behold!

If anyone hears My voice,
And will open, open, open the door, I will come in.

It was almost bedtime when we thought we heard a knock at the door. Before we could answer, there was a second, much louder knock. It got our attention! Dad looked out the window. He saw it was our neighbor and quickly opened the door.

A knock gets your attention. It also requires a decision. Will you open the door or not? Sometimes Jesus wants to get our attention. He has something to say. He wants to be our Savior. So He gets our attention, just like a knock at the door. Has Jesus ever knocked on the door of your heart? When He does, you must decide. Please let Jesus into your heart!

Word Watch

Behold, I stand at the door and knock; if anyone hears My voice and opens the door, I will come in to him and will dine with him, and he with Me.

Revelation 3:20 NAS3

Let
Jesus
into
your
heart

MY PRAYER FOR TODAY

Father, my heart is like a door. You knock, asking to come in.
May I always open the door. Amen.

Uphold Me!

And when I fall, the Lord will pick me up.

You are walking along just fine. Then suddenly you fall. If you skin an elbow or knee, it hurts. It can be hard to get back up. That's when we need a friend to "uphold us." A friend must care. He must be strong and make sure you're all right. Then he helps you up . . . he *up*holds you.

When you walk with the Lord, you do things that please Him. You read your Bible and pray. But then, something happens; you "fall." When we "fall," we disappoint God. Maybe we act unkind. Maybe we stop praying. But Jesus is our friend! He *up*holds us when we fall. He is strong and makes sure we are all right. He helps us get back up and on our way with Him!

Word Watch

The LORD upholds all those who fall and lifts up all who are bowed down.

Psalm 145:14

The
Lord
is
strong

MY PRAYER FOR TODAY

Father, when I am weak, You are strong. Uphold me when I fall. Amen.

Now I Lay Me Down to Sleep

Now I lay me down to sleep.
I pray my soul You'll keep.

There is a very important word in this bedtime prayer. It is the word *now*. It tells us the best time to talk with God is right now. So many times we put off saying our prayers. We may be too tired. Sometimes we just forget. After tending sheep all day, David the shepherd boy was very tired. But he always found time to pray.

He said, "On my bed, I remember You, Lord." David remembered that God loved him *now*. That God would take care of him, right now and all through the night. He could have waited for another day to pray. But now was the right time for David. Now is the right time for us too! God is always listening for you!

Word Watch

On my bed I remember you; I think of you through the watches of the night.

Psalm 63:6

~

The
best
time
to
pray
is
now

MY PRAYER FOR TODAY

Father, now is the best time to pray. Amen.